What We Did
With Old Moons

By M.V. Montgomery

Winter Goose
Publishing

Winter Goose Publishing
2701 Del Paso Road, 130-92
Sacramento, CA 95835

www.wintergoosepublishing.com
Contact Information: info@wintergoosepublishing.com

What We Did With Old Moons
COPYRIGHT © 2012 by M.V. Montgomery
First Edition, November 2012
ISBN 978-0-9881845-4-1

Cover Image & Background by Doug Cockell
Cover Design by Winter Goose Publishing
Typeset by Michelle Lovi

Published in the United States of America

To Nardi T.,
who walked on
the moon with me.

Table of Contents

i

MYTHOS

There were dinosaurs
left over from the Jurassic era
at that time,
known as dragons.
And the Neanderthal
lingered on,
inspiring tales
of wild men and yeti.

Back then,
you could pick up precious stones
from the hillsides
or scoop handfuls of gold
out of a stream.
Everywhere
a rainbow touched
lay a fortune.

And the old kings
built monuments
to themselves,
but in the absence of writing,
their names were lost.
Soon it was forgotten
whether they were once
mortals or gods.

WHAT WE DID WITH OLD MOONS

The full moon always made a satisfying draught. We used to say, *Here's moon in your eye!* or sip some and remark, *That's good moon.* We loved our moon then, would slice it like pie, use it for custards and cakes, or pour it into children's milk—not much, though, lest they become moody as teens. And it made a good beard silverer, tooth brightener, and a fine eye-glow. The white white was so remarkable we lined streets with it to see better at dusk, slapped just a dash on corners here and there, spread it evenly over fences. And we needed it, because we'd have to wait twenty-eight days until the next moon harvest. We knew if we didn't embrace that fullness while we could, it'd go to waste, break into shards and dissipate into the night sky, too bright to form clouds but too thin for stars. So we'd take our milk buckets and meet in the meadow, where the men murmured and mixed their paint while the women brushed highlights into their hair. And the moon-maids laughed and filled their pails while the boys positioned their ladders and scampered up oh so daringly close! They would see who could climb right next to that old satellite, come down coated in beams, ready to chase or be chased in a game of moon-tag. And you'd know when you were caught, because the light left circles on your skin and mantles in your hair and lunules on all of your fingertips. But we didn't care—we bathed in it, knew it must wear off soon, before the new moon cast its spell. Until then, we were all lunar children, lambent-eyed and laughing, lost in our moon-foolishness.

OUR OLD GODS

Oh, we had many more gods in those days! There was one old fellow
responsible for thunder, Old Break-a-Lung we called him. And a god
for a thin red sunrise, Sareen we called her, saying, *That's just the tip
of her tiara, now, surely she'll be up soon.* And there was another god
of the fallen-firework kind of sunset we called Nek-a-Nek. We'd say,
*Old Nek-a-Nek has broken his tray of eggs again, look at that mess,
won't Black Stan be put to some trouble trying to sweep all that up!*
And we had a god for helping you along on your journey we called
Allatone. If you came to a fork in the road, you'd pick up a handful
of pebbles and spin around and let them go, and wherever Allatone
caught them, in that direction you would trust. Though some said
he had a ghost dog that could generate gusts of wind by snapping at
the stones, which sometimes put you off course.

And we had a god for the feeling of being followed, Prying Matilda
as she was known, and a god for the sudden feeling of freedom in
open spaces we called Tippiyuma. I guess that may just have been
the kind of thing you felt like yelling in that situation, *Tippi-yuma!*
And we had a god for mending fences we called Handy Megg and
a god to watch the kids when you weren't there, Grueclaws, although
this Grueclaws was rather benign, having a reputation of being too
matronly. So for unruly kids you might cast a binding spell through
Kaleestra, whom you had to be extra-careful with because there was
always a quid pro quo. In exchange for a handful of scared-straight kids
you might get a broken pot, or a persistent wailing emanating through
your walls at night.

And we had gods with extra limbs, and two heads, and at least one with his head on backwards, and several gods with parts of animals and parts of men and women. And gods who could make you feel better, and gods who made your enemies feel worse, and tokens you could swallow just like medicine to cure any ills, or to sing more eloquently in choir, or to come up with a conversational topper in a storytelling bout at the bar. And wherever you went, you could always take your army of icons along like a boy his toy soldiers, and you could spread them all out and it felt just like that—like having an army at your own beck and call. And you never felt lonely with so many gods around—gods on the end-table, or in bookcases, or standing still with lampshade hats on their heads. Or under your bed, or in pillow feathers whispering into your ear while you slept, or in every sweet exhalation of your breath. Oh, we were god-rich then! I miss it at times, often wish I could recall where I packed my icons away. But I have grown old, and this world you see around you is a much different place.

WHAT WE DID IN SPRING

When the rains stopped, we'd take the Harvest Man down
from the hayloft, where he'd stared forlornly into the rafters
for months with his moss-grown eyes and daddy longlegs lashes.
Oh, you hollow bag of bones! Oh, you stick-and-figure man!
we taunted. We young people replaced his eyes with acorns
and smeared his lips with purple berries. Then we raised the
motley old effigy up on a pole and carried it house to house,
demanding our tribute of sweets and seeds, singing all the while.

Later, we marched that pole over the fresh-turned fields and
planted it in the earth. We adorned it with daisies and ivy.
Then each of us caught an end of a curling vine and danced,
and the songs carried on all afternoon—*Soon, a Little More*
or *Ashes to Ashes*. At dusk, we reconvened to burn down
the Harvest Man and to feast on our plunder, roasting treats
over the rotted straw hulk with its sagging mouth and doleful
eye sockets. Chanting as we did, *Harvest is dead, all must be fed.*

In due course, a Lord and Lady were chosen. Their attendants
prepared a bower of green leaves and flower petals and arranged
lit candles in a circle. Then we skipped away across the furrows,
two-by-two, scattering dark handfuls of seeds. Lord and Lady
were left alone in that meadow as the candles winked on and off like
fairy-lights—left to stretch tentative hands toward one another,
left to discover new love.

THE PARALLEL UNIVERSES

Good heavens, yes, there are parallel universes! More, I'll wager, than you, or I, or anyone else could possibly count. Sometimes I'll catch myself running in two directions at once and we'll both look over at the same time and nod, *There's Me!* I guess that's one for the philosophers to sort out. Or, when I'm running a little short of cash, I'll catch a wealthier Self passing by a portal and maybe hit myself up for a loan. Lots of advantages, you know, to so many universes—and to think, when I was younger, we were content with just the one! We were ignorant children, of course, hardly better than the old Flat-Earthers or Jerusalem-Centrists. Things are better this way. You can keep yourself company, enjoy the comfort of knowing there's plenty of Me out there to go around whenever you feel like maybe you've stretched yourself too thin.

Funny thing, though—when you reflect that you are everywhere simultaneously, you do become less inclined to waste so much time or money on yourself. Because you think, *Well, now, I could eat a second helping, but there's probably another Me starving somewhere in a Slum World, poor kid, and I'm having a pretty good year when all's said and done.* Even when things aren't going so well, you can't help but think, *Look, there's probably some poor Me running around out there with his head cut off, or who's been framed for some petty offense in a Rough Cop World, I should count my lucky stars!*

And who's to say there aren't places even worse than those we can imagine ourselves? That humans aren't being sacrificed right now in a Cannibal World across the street, or in a Reptile-Ruled Kingdom, just over your shoulder? No thank you, I'll stick with the good old Earth, as strip-mined and untidy as it is—it's my home, it's where I was brought up, call me Old School. Certainly, I can't help gazing at the stars when they appear, and wonder just like anyone else if there isn't a Peace-Garden Universe or perhaps a Chocolate Planet or even (I blush to say this) a Heaven. Like I said before, Old School. I apologize for running on a bit, however. You children get along—I imagine you've someplace better to be.

THE FLOWER PEOPLE

The Flower People were everywhere in that era. Some called them
fairies, some pixies—to be honest, I never could discern the difference.
They flocked in such great numbers they'd leave their dust everywhere,
and you had to be careful not to inhale too long because then you'd get
lightheaded and perhaps even float a little off the ground. Of course,
we teenagers just loved that, would park our bikes in the meadow just
to breathe and soar on a cloud all night.

That was when the tide turned against fairies in our town. Soon we were
forced to fill holes in hollow trees with cement and uproot pond-lilies from
the muck. A mistake. It wasn't long before we missed their singing—
it wasn't that rubbery sound of cicadas or a high-pitched shrilling, more
a soft wind-sighing with tinkling bells.

Yes, summer never sounded quite the same afterwards. I miss the fairies,
sometimes wonder where they went. Some say the mountains, some say
the ice floes. Some say they are out there still, just doing a better job of
staying hidden. That their camouflage wings evolved past the level of the
stick or leaf insects, becoming altogether invisible, which is a miracle
of adaptation we human beings could learn something from!

Others say the fairies dwell in cloud cities and drop down only rarely for
a nighttime caucus, gathering around a ring of toadstools. Or that they
occasionally ride past us on butterflies, and the excess weight is what
makes those insects swoop and dip in that peculiar way they do: *A fairy
just hopped aboard!* as we liked to say.

I can't tell: I was never too adept at spotting them, you see, even as an impressionable child. In fact, I recall only one Flower Child sighting. She was nesting in a bed of violets when I bent over to take a sniff. Frightened at being awakened, she rose up out of the petals, spun her arms in a flash of light, and was gone.

THE SULLEN

Bah! All you kids recognize are the monsters right in front of your faces. Camera hogs. Plastic confections with glue. In my day, monsters lurked alone on the fringes of the community. They were sullen and had serious father issues, but they knew their job was to keep you in line, which they accomplished without resorting to special effects. I recall one fellow, Bog Karl we used to call him, who lived in a marsh area where teenagers liked to hold parties. When things got too loud for his liking, he'd reach up from the ooze with snake-arms and pull one down, no questions asked, maybe just a bubble to mark someone's final scream. And another real character, Old Titch we called her, had long tree-limb fingers to poke you if you attempted to sneak out of your window at night. If you knew what was good for you, you'd head straight back into bed and say your prayers! At the quarry stood the Guardians, stone giants who emerged out of cliffs to crush hikers who climbed where they didn't belong. At the very least, you could bet they'd send a shower of rocks your way. So you always had to be on your toes. Sometimes if you heard a little rumble and glanced up, you could just catch a glimpse of craggy heads and grim mouths frowning upon humankind in utter disdain. Perhaps you would observe to a friend, *You see, doesn't that look just like a face up there?* But those titans could be tricky, blending back instantly like double-exposed images into the rock. That's why I said earlier, all the monsters we used to have were stealthy, vanishing into shadows when you flipped on a light switch or sang a hymn. They had no use for quick startles, or hanging-eyeball or melted-face masks. But they really knew how to work a room, and left behind a feeling of unease that stayed with you for a long, long time. I guess that's why they call it a *good* scare—you'd remember Bog Karl or Old Titch and think *No, best play it safe, it's not worth the risk, give me that straight and narrow path every time.*

SO MANY WITCHES

Black
pool of water.
A gourd.
A traffic cone.
The sharpness
in a cat's eyes.
Knit scarf,
knotted.
Jagged row
of coat toggles.
In a corner
by the furnace,
a broom.

Brown
packaging paper.
The letter *W.*
The winter wind.
Dark bluffs
dotted with
unidentified lights.
Animal shriek
amid
barren trees.
Shadow
moving past
the moon.

IN MY TIME

In my time, vampires weren't beloved of teens and certainly never smiled. They had henchmen with faces like voles who'd pack their coffins and cart them from castle to town. Then at nighttime, they would rise up and create more holy terror. Vampires dressed like they were off to cocktail parties, but were notoriously close-lipped so you couldn't see their fangs. Possibly, they were self-conscious about their Eastern European accents. Mostly, they just leered significantly and floated around in the midst of other guests. And they always gave off a dank smell and hissed at you like a cat if you came in too close. Then you'd know what you had!

In my time, mad scientists were the true venture capitalists. Sure they were evil, always plotting expansion and world domination, yet also risk-takers, pioneers, applied scientists with their advanced degrees in electro-physical-chemistry just waiting for their big break. They could send a jolt through a cadaver until it sat up on a table, head attached or not. And very typically they'd have a hunchback in their employ, resourceful blokes dispatched to fetch more body parts just like you'd send someone to the store for cigarettes. True, this might mean disturbing a freshly dug grave, but no harm there: the dead are the dead, as far as I'm concerned.

In my time, you could find mummy cases at any natural history museum, but these were always disappointing, offering cutaway-bubble glimpses of faces blackened like catfish. If you were on a class field trip, it was easy to scoff and say, *I'm not afraid*, but of course, some bully might hold you there after the others had left and threaten to seal you in the tomb where no one could ever find you. So that was a slightly different proposition. Who knows, maybe then the life force really could be sucked out of you by the bandaged body underneath, and the stiffened arms might unfurl. And you'd hear a dusty voice complain aloud, *Who disturbs my sleep?*

THE NIGHT SKY

Back then you could see things clearer at night, sharp enough to count
the points on stars or the rings on planets. And satellites looked just like
holiday ornaments; in fact, the whole firmament was lit up like Christmas,
with clouds of purple-and-green gas and blood-red meteors streaking off
into the distance. With respect to UFOs—those were better defined, also,
which is how anyone understood what they were. Most were shaped like
saucers, milk-white silver with hatch-rings in the center. Of course, even
in those days, the aliens just performed flyovers. I think we must have
disappointed them, badly, back in the pyramid-building times, as soon as
they perceived how warlike and intractable we were, really no better than
a herd of cats, and not worth their bother. Our disappointed parents, you
might say. Pity, because they were a gentle Pythagorean race themselves,
bulb heads, olive skin, with eyes just as sweet as any cow's. These days,
when I look into the night sky and see a bright blip of light, or can imagine
I hear a heavenly resonance quite beyond the din of our cell phone signals
and other beamed nonsense, I have to wonder whether an intelligent race
will ever look down upon us again and declare, *Ah, it's been a long time
now, and there are always evolutionary miracles. Maybe it's finally time
to give those poor apes another chance?*

MY OLD SCHOOL

At my Old School all the happy nefarities were never too far out of sight, the intellectual gamesmanship and gambling with futures, most occurring in and around the Midway. You'd see freaky people, paradigm-setters, word-swallowers, idea jugglers, and, crowned in mortarboard and sporting a watch-fob, the Dean of Fools. There were rides, too, that reliable old Trivium which sent you spinning three directions at once, sideways and up-ways and counter-clock-ways, the Barely-Go-Round which made your head spin, and over-coasters which left you grasping at air. And you'd scream with your group of peers, swearing if you all lived through this, never again, but the raw dose of reality wouldn't last, and oftentimes you'd see the worst complainers filing out one gate and lining up quickly at the next. Gluttons for punishment, fools. And the barkers would try to brow-beat you into playing games with near-impossible odds, but really they were just trying to wise you up. They'd hand you back a ball saying, *Here, can't you feel it, it's weighted, we can calculate the trajectory if you'd like,* flipping over a chart and talking swiftly to hold your interest. Or to be heard above the music, because always rides were noisy, some with string quartets standing nearby or blowsy bagpipes or choral groups singing scales as erstwhile academic climbers assailed the library stacks. Think what you will of the thudding rhythms of today, just enough out of synch with your heartbeat to unsettle you, and so loud that you start to lose focus and believe the blood is being piped into you from outside: I still say, there is nothing more frightful than a good operatic murmur as you wend your way through a haunted tunnel filled with theatre people, or knowing that you must stand up to the Debate Club on the square, else be put in stocks. That's what colleges lack today, that old agony-ecstasy and abiding sense of shame. In my day, it was a hard job to Fool the Guesser and you knew the campus swarmed with carnies just itching to con you; still you accepted all this humbly, believing you too were part of the show.

THE DISOBEDIENT ZONE

In the Disobedient Zone, you often saw lonely children walking down highway shoulders, left to journey on alone by their parents. Some with smirks or cross-eyes, because petulance sticks to a child's face forever. Some with sassy tongues sticking out of their heads they couldn't retract, or rotting or missing teeth from their uncontrollable candy obsessions! Others clearly hadn't heeded adult warnings about bb-gun backfires and resembled pirates with black eye patches. Or had heads on backwards from unsupervised acrobatics on backyard trampolines, or deep wounds from scabs they just never could stop picking. And oh yes, you could see zombies shuffling by with sucker sticks poking out through the backs of their heads or sharp scissors through their chests, and there was always an unpleasant moaning sound rising from somewhere below the vestibule. You knew kids down there must've committed far more serious crimes against their parents and were now grounded forever, which is to say grounded literally, in caves where they could never ever watch TV again or be visited by their friends. No, we didn't have those video games in your grandpa's day, but I'm sure the consequences of overplaying those must be dire, say permanently jerky arms and elongated thumbs. We did have kids who contracted google-eyes from squinting too long at TV, with burned-out red holes where their retinas should have been. So my advice to you all is to go outside while the sun is still shining, and play.

THREE URBAN LEGENDS

Ladon

We knew something was out there in the lake, just past the docks, and it
wouldn't do to turn your back as twilight approached because one lash
of a tail might send you plunging, and cold coils would squeeze tight as
the mirror of the world closed overhead. Even on a bright day, you might
believe you'd miscounted a row of ducks, or observe a sudden swell and
perhaps query aloud, *Too big for a fish, and I don't recall seeing a boat?*
Down, down, under algae and reeds an entity wound side to side, eel-like,
but with jagged teeth that could shred a fish or slice a bite out of a canoe
just like it was a cantaloupe! Police divers might see an accretion of junk
and think nothing amiss, might pass by the curved shape nestling inside
a sunken boat hull or the bulge beneath a ripped canvass of a sail. Soon
origin stories proliferated of a tropical pet flushed down a pipe, subsisting
in sewers and eventually migrating to the lake, somehow surviving in
the warmer reaches as winter ice knit together above its head. And this
unwillingly trapped being, denied its childhood under the sun, forsaken,
left to subsist on garbage and never encountering another of its kind, grew
into a monster, thumping its frozen casement angrily and vowing revenge,
come spring, upon any living creature unlucky enough to swim by.

Minos

Above the Plaza was the giant head of a bull. When department stores filled and registers got humming, it registered approval by blowing smoke out its nose. And that particular mall was a confusing one to navigate, but at the door you could rent a fishing reel of twine to unspool as you made your way through the concourse. Of course, this was no help sometimes, on a busy weekend, if the thread became confounded with other shoppers'. You could always expect to see a group of old men sitting around on benches in the atrium arguing over a huge string-ball that grew larger and larger as they talked. Woe to those caught wandering past closing time, because back then there weren't warnings over the intercom like today's, just banks of lights snapping off and shopkeepers rolling their gates shut to guard against marauders and security hounds. They say mall dogs are the most vicious, and I'd have to agree: can you imagine, caged up all day, hearing appalling tunes designed to lure patrons to founder on sales racks, literally thousands of intruders flaunting their presence just off-camera, seniors and wailing babies and good-for-nothing teens—why, it'd be enough to drive a canine insane! And so we heard tales of people lost and never heard from again, and you can bet those hounds cleaned their plates.

Woodwose

Always we were warned about him, that shadowy figure reputed to live by
the parkway in the bird sanctuary, a wild man who defended his territory
from teens parking too late by grimacing outside windshields and giving
everyone a fright. He ate out of trash cans, they all said, which might have
explained the look of sour bitterness on his face, though by nature he was
a misanthrope and half-hater of himself. That other part, according to
speculation, might have been orangutan, because his face was covered
with gold hair and two lower teeth broke through his lip when he tried to
speak. Whether words were possible was an open question, since it was
more of a sad lowing that you might hear when the Old Moon and hearts
grew full, carrying off the lake surface, always shining so brightly below,
like a silver paten! A howl of despair, but also one of lonely freedom,
which was what adults half-admired when they drove past and recalled
stories they had once heard as children. For here was a being who had
simplified life—career, home, family, society—by pushing it all away.

EXPLORE THE CONTINENT OF YOURSELF

Explore the continent of yourself, while you are young. Go on pilgrimages
through deserts, hack your way through jungles, take calculated risks, swear all
for love. Balloon over impediments until they fade into a patchwork below.

Let the waves crash over you, let dolphins ferry you far past the Dardanelles,
avoid the antipodes where life cannot abide long. Learn to navigate by sheer will.
Leave maps of the terrain and steer by stars, using intuition as your astrolabe.

Write, report back. Plan your next expedition, make charts, be accountable for
all members of your team. Settle an isle as solitary as you can stand, then
build your compound. Clear and plant and refashion and shape. Finally, at some

blessed point you may reach, when finances are seen to and the kids are all right,
set sail once more, like Ulysses, past the known world, past blank spaces on maps
where monsters and leviathans spout. Lend your wisdom to a worth cause—

then drop off the end of the earth, and remember yourself as you are.

THE SLEEPWALKERS

The sleepwalkers emerge like Lazarus,
eyelids aflutter,
walking their stiff-kneed limps.

They hunger for more sleep,
foreheads still warm from the pillow
and their flattened visions.

The sleepwalkers search for missing pieces
of their lives,
strive to reconnect but remain adrift,
like just so many sculls at sea.

They yearn for clairvoyance,
or inexpressible truth,
or perhaps love.

The sleepwalkers remember bits and pieces
of their habitats, which are richer for
their half-imagined dimensions.

They listen
as the house settles and water flows
through the walls.

The sleepwalkers bump into the unseen
and therefore remain
quite tranquil and whole.

They are stripped down to themselves,
the original peoples,
while the rest of history is a dream.

MY PROFILE

I'm a morning person, at least when I need to be. It's true—that's when I get the most work done. I'm a night person, too, often an insomniac, sometimes with ideas I can't put to rest, or a nightstand book that's made me think (and then, too late to shut things down!). Sensitive Virgin and Stolid Ox—if those signs cohere logically for you. They don't for me. I may be a ruminant in philosophy, but not always in my daily practice. Socially liberal, fiscally conservative—rare to meet someone who *isn't*. I've resided long enough in the South to have picked up a twang, but I lose it quickly when around my *Fargo*-speaking friends. I'm Minnesota-nice, usually, and blond, but not Scandinavian. Would you believe it, Italian and French, with just a little German and Scots-Irish for coloring. Does this suggest an inner tempest? A passionate Mediterranean side? Ask my students to describe me, they might say, *he's a stickler*. Others say *take him, he's easy, easy to talk to*. But what am I predominantly, then, when I'm finally at home, or when no one's looking? Isn't that the essential test? No clear-cut answer there—a tree-falls-in-the-forest poser. As Stendahl wrote, the only thing one can't form in solitude is character. And those personality tests only further confuse things. Am I a leader, an agreeable people-person, a reclusive-creative sort? Yes, yes, and yes—so we all must be. A follower-parent? A worker-misanthrope? An artist-extrovert? If those are alternatives, then they must form unstable bonds, at least in this universe. Montaigne had it right: we humans are all just a mess of contradictions. Even the Zen ideal of present-living is just that, an ideal. Who wants to subsist on the bare level of biological necessity, or stimulus-response? I know that when I'm cleaning the floor, I don't want to think about cleaning the floor. I want to be composing something wonderful just wonderful in my head. When I drive to work, I want to be contemplating my retirement fund. By now you get the idea—I hate to be pinned down. I hate to see anyone try to pin *you* down. I'm a Type-A, a Type-B, and a Type-C. I'm reserved as any busy person can reasonably claim to be, safeguarding my solitude, at least when I'm not commuting or entertaining kids on weekends. Things can get pretty hairy then. But I like order & chaos. I also enjoy the city & the outdoors, though I can't help recall Emerson's words about men always professing to love Nature. I'm just not so sure I can rightfully claim a love above others', can you? Some people believe that our personalities may be traceable to blood type, ultimately, but at an appointment recently, I discovered I'd forgotten mine. So I might be a universal donor or a universal recipient. How about you?

PAINT IT BLACK

It was not easy having a monk for an older brother,
one who never misbehaved, one who practiced
asceticism from an early age, refusing most treats.
Saying he didn't need anything at the Dairy Queen,
Save your money Mom and Dad. Or hitching up his
pants with a *Don't worry, these will last just fine.*
His incident reports always lined up a chain of facts
that stopped at me. While, lagging two years behind,
I had trouble telling a story straight, with too much
of my father's gift for hyperbole.

My mother considered Santa Claus a Catholic agent,
one who yearly placed an Abel's sacrifice of gifts
beneath the tree for my brother, knock-offs in a
Cain-pile for me. My brother got the scale-model
race car to ride in, mine was a plastic toddler toy.
He got the Stars jersey, mine was the Black Hawks.
He got the Vikings helmet with foam lining, mine
was a red shell with star from a discount-store team
that didn't play actual games. He got the Beatles
and I got the Rolling Stones.

In midlife, when I tried to compete with others'
tales of transgressions, I found myself outmatched.
My rebellion had consisted of holing up downstairs,
reading instead of joining the family circle at the TV,
playing LPs as loud as I could on my cheap speakers.
That Christmas, as I made my exit to play the Stones,

heard *"Smiling faces I look and see / but not for me,"*
I thought, for the first time, *The Beatles are for sissies.*
Then I pictured my brother by the tree, helmeted,
smile stretched around a mouth guard,

proudly holding up a rainbow-colored football with
kicking tee: Good Boy Awards. I had unwrapped
a football too, plain speckled pigskin. But on it was
an official NFL logo that gleamed like a forbidden fruit.
Content now, I held the ball under my arm and watched
the record spin. Then had a second first-ever thought:
My brother is a sissy, too. In that moment, it did not
seem so bad to be of the Devil's party. True, I did not
think the matter through. I just knew I could not walk
a line straight from Santa to God.

LIVES PARALLAX

In another universe, you had an extra brother,
and your godfather wasn't killed in a plane crash,
and your brother didn't bury his first child,
and someone near to you wasn't an abuser.

In a second universe, you did, after all,
get your first girlfriend pregnant, then married her,
and lived in a rock-and-roll house full of kids.
You also managed a restaurant.

Against all odds, yours was the marriage
others looked up to and thought, *rock solid*,
and your wife stayed busy with her curtain-hanging business
while you became the sad sack of your bowling team.

There is a third universe to consider. Because
had you been just a little bit bolder, or more rash,
you might have dropped out to pursue a career as a writer.
Here there are two possible splinter paths.

In one, you are observed seated at a table
and the words don't come, and perhaps
there is a bottle in the vicinity, and you are in denial
about the cliché your whole life has become.

In the other, you are reading script after script
in a high-rise office and wondering if you have done
the right thing by coming to this strange place,
and hoping that you have. Because

there is always a chance a meeting will come and you
will be able to slip your own script into the pile
under a plausible-sounding alias. And perhaps
one of those brass fasteners in the impeccably

hole-punched draft will momentarily catch a glint
of LA sun, and then finally find the producer's eye.
And he will ask suddenly, apropos of nothing,
What about that one?

FRANK O'HARA

Sometimes it's important
to face down
those Academy poets,

look them in the eye,
let them know
you mean business.

There's nothing wrong
with becoming a concierge
of your own experience,

like warning the audience
at Universal Studios Tours

O keep your heads up!
at the moment of attack,
but allowing them

the comfort of knowing
they were in safe hands,
all along.

SEASONAL

Hooves pound
unceasingly

atop the tomato,
or *tomahto*.

Equestrian statues
turn their heads,

releasing
hard riders.

The fallen heroes
adjust their tune—

hoplites
of an afternoon.

LINCOLN'S POCKETS

They held his
his wallet,
with pouches
for "U.S. Currency,"
"Railroad Tickets,"
and "Notes"

a pencil,
for jotting down
text for speeches

nine news clippings
favorable
to his policies

a Confederate
five-dollar bill,
perhaps
a souvenir
of the recent fall
of Richmond

his pocket knife,
ivory and silver,
surprisingly delicate,
much used

one sleeve button

his gold watch fob,
the kind of thing
any person might
lose if not
tucked away

his glasses,
to which he
had made
a humble repair
with a string

a replacement pair,
as a precaution,
in case this repair
did not hold

a lens polisher
and a buffer,

and a linen handkerchief
with its simple
red monogram:
A. Lincoln.

IV

HOSTAGES FOR CHRISTMAS

Counting

Winter was the season in which we always seemed to be counting. Whether this was because the falling snow was a more apportioned monotony than sun or rain, or because of the steady drip of icicles and the way they would attenuate with age like ice beards, or because one day followed another like its exact unthawed copy to be held preserved into the next—but we were always counting. In school we made paper-chain calendars, each rolled link a day for one of the days until Christmas, and Nance and I would begin to look forward to when Grandpa and Grandma Gallanti drove up from Lincoln, Nebraska, to visit. We would wait on the hill where the Knowlans used to live to watch for green cars coming around the bend, for the one green car that would separate from the trough of snow in its lane and pull towards our side. Usually Steve Eaves joined us, too. Steve could act really strange around Nance, and I wonder now whether it was on my account he sat out with us, or rather if, by ignoring Nance as athletically as possible—sliding down the back and dragging me with him, I hollering because a likely-looking car might just be turning the corner—he wasn't simply trying to impress her, at an age when all direct attention-paying was taboo.

The Knowlan house

We had an unspoken agreement not to wait farther down the street than the Knowlan house. The yard had a taller embankment than any others on our street, plus a view of the corner. The way the noise of passing cars was hushed made it seem like there was glass between them and us, through which our voices, after glancing off garages or the trunks of stripped elms like fence- or sounding-boards lining the street, passed unimpeded. It was quiet, like you imagined it would be inside the bubbles of broken watches or stopped clocks. The house was beige, usually abandoned by its most recent tenant before the harsh winter. We still called it the Knowlan house because the Knowlans had lived in it for three years. As for the time Nance and I spent waiting there, or rather, for the seconds we trimmed off Gram and Grandpa's trip by waiting there instead of at our house, that mattered little. Perhaps it was really only my and Nance's way of signaling to them, wherever we fancied they were at the time, that we hoped it might be down the street next to ours; or though we could not meet them halfway, we could at least meet them partway, however meager a fraction of the distance ours was.

A sign

And so we would wait in the Knowlan yard, where the departure of the most recent tenant usually created a need for a For Rent sign in the snow, the realtor's name, DON FOSSE, swinging on the attached nameplate below. Steve Eaves and I threw snowballs "at Don Fosse," trying to make the panel trapeze back and forth. Nance spoke of the realtor as though he were a titan doll of hers whom she imagined striding across people's yards. And as we heard the smaller sign click in the breeze, we perceived it marked off the seconds for us. Because we were always counting.

Lost tourists

Grandpa of course knew Steve, always asking whether he and Nance had set the date yet, after a car had suddenly detached from the others and turned into our street—honking repeatedly, assertively. Grandpa would twist over to Gram's side so he could roll open her window. Then he would say:

"Well halloo there young strangers, excuse me please. My mother and I are lost."

"You see," he paused, "we went out this morning for a four hundred-mile drive and we're from Nebraska, and our two grandchildren and their friend were supposed to meet us right here so we can go to their house and commence Christmas, but the little rascals ..."

The steam from all the breath and pretending obscured itself into his white hair, and Gram who could never wait and never wait to use the bathroom beamed as she hushed him, rosy, trying to say hellos and blow kisses to all of us simultaneously. We had all slid down to the sidewalk, I headfirst in a bid to try to beat Nance, but inwardly relieved to be jumped upon and held down by Steve and to feel Nance pass, laughing and less shy, continuing to laugh as she ran up to the car door, opened it, and dove inside, landing on Gram's lap with a wet whump of the snowsuit. Gram, whose face was all exploded like she'd just been dealt three aces and couldn't hide it, but with mixed pain, because no thanks to Nance's mad bouncing she could just barely hold herself a minute longer.

Horsing around

Grandpa hollered, "I believe we are under attack!" in mock amazement, shaking hands all around, however, with the children who had grown and stretched themselves (he said) out of all recognition. He snatched Nance up under his arm, never letting her go until he had carried her up to our doorstep and tested her thighs with several prize-turkey pinches before ceremoniously presenting her to Mother, "to be stuffed and roasted in the oven immediately."

Nance would be screaming "No!" in delight and Mother would kiss her as though it was her daughter, not her father, whom she hadn't seen in a year. And Grandpa remarked that he far preferred gobbling a turkey to hearing one gobble, so if Mother liked, he could just wring the bird's neck now. But he didn't mean it.

We all jumped into the car and helped drive, showing Gram and Grandpa the way to our house while getting the capsule summary of the trip from Gram. And a warning from Grandpa that we'd all better simmer down now, because we had gotten so big we would bust the car in half, and if that happened, blood relatives or not, he would have us all in the hoosegow for Christmas. But we didn't think he meant that, either.

It was all so fast and immediate. We paraded down the block, Grandpa bellowing or singing "Jingle Bells" like a drunken man, the car jerking because he was alternately pressing the brake and accelerator. It was all so quick Nance and I forgot that a few moments before, we had been counting. The hill, locked in long hibernation under a deep layer of snow, became the place where we would expect to find Christmas again next year.

Harry

When the Knowlans moved in, I was only six years old. Same age as Harry, whom I remember now as an adopted kid with orange hair, a queerly adult kind of voice, and something else. He had a disquieting character trait that would have counted for a virtue among grown-people, and which at any other age might have hinted at precocious-ness, but at the time seemed to signal the opposite, almost a genetic deficiency. For Harry never ever lied, which at that age was as simple as saying what your favorite color was, or where you lived, or how many members you had in your family. My mother was never very fond of either Mr. or Mrs. Knowlan. Mr. Knowlan worked for the Army, and perhaps she felt that because it would only be a matter of time before he was restationed, she might avoid the personal invest-ment required to be anything more than just neighborly. When he was home, I recall Mr. Knowlan's bass voice calling down the block for Harry, who would tense up either to the sound, or to the habitual inspection threatened in such bi-syllabic bullets as "Harry!" or "Sup-per!" He would remain afloat for a while in a kind of supplicatory silence before leaving, hoping to elicit a promise from me and Steve or Phil and Dan Crowder of what we would do the next day.

Forewarned

Once I was sitting on the sofa in our living room when my mother stormed in from the kitchen, where she had just been talking on the phone with Mrs. Knowlan. Now she was furious. Not at me, though apparently Harry had come home bawling from a kick in the groin or a whack from a plastic bat—not at me, but at Mrs. Knowlan, who had been letting her have it. Mother had too sour a taste from the receiver to punish me, or as too prepossessed with a larger struggle, perhaps seeing my transgression as an allied blow in the War Against Knowlan. Instead of spanking me, she sat me down and held me by the arm, warning me to keep away from the Knowlan's yard, telling me that Mr. and Mrs. Knowlan were the kind of people who "stole children." I had been forewarned early about these; strangers who lured little children into their cars with promises of candy or toys, then drove them away—forever.

War

At the time, our mother's warnings were almost mythological in their hold over Nance and me. I remember not daring to walk over circular depressions in lawns where she said wells had been, but were now covered over. Mother cited several instances of kids who had done so, falling through sunken topsoil and rotted planks to drown or pray to God for rescue, remaining in water and darkness for hours. She had been a witness on the day Uncle Gino and a friend had saved a small Italian girl in their Chicago neighborhood. Gino was just ten. According to our family legend, The Friend held Gino's legs while Gino grabbed both of the girl's hands, then The Friend and Gino combined their strength to pull her out. They are each holding an arm around the girl and grinning (probably because the photographer has just asked them to put their arms around a girl) in the yellowed newspaper picture.

"Don't the police try to get Mr. and Mrs. Knowlan?" I asked, wide-eyed.

"I don't know. Just you keep away from them, and out of their yard, so they don't steal *you*."

That was all: war was on against the Knowlans. But for an instant I imagined myself in Harry's place as it must have been when the car door slammed shut and the block where he belonged rushed away in the window. And that night I dreamed that for once I had beaten Nance into Gram and Grandpa's car, but the hand that reached around me to shut the door was ghostly white, not Grandpa's but Mrs. Knowlan's. I awoke feeling sorry for Harry, my unpunished sin of the day before still unerased, unabsolved, to haunt me not just one night, but to buoy up often during the times we played together.

Steve and I and the Crowders did continue to include Harry in some of our strategic plans, though the War Against Knowlan continued between our parents until the Knowlans moved away—too often giving us an excuse for whatever devilry we cared to perpetrate, because we knew we could get away with it.

Believer

I hadn't stopped believing yet. Because though each Christmas passed by without me getting what I really wanted and had asked about for as long as I could recall (I was seven), to stop believing would have been to forsake once and for all a long relied- and prevailed-upon source of hope and magic. So I would as soon have given up on Santa now as an old magician would have snapped his wand or tossed aside his old felt rabbit-engendering hat after their years of service. Especially this year; I felt that somehow, this would be the year. I sensed even before it was done that beyond lie the brink and span of a time-creased world of experience in which expectations were trained to center upon the object of desire and whittle it out slowly, never all at once, and so you could never have things all at once either, though that is the way you continued to want them.

A spell

I imagined that through sheer strength of longing I could put myself under a spell, what Aunt Jess would have called a "cantrip," calculated to yield up the one present I wrote to Santa, and prayed to God for. This Christmas, the amalgam of all my past years' wishing and disappointment was welling up around me mysteriously, like steam from a readying cauldron. I hypnotized myself, dreaming each waking moment was part of a formula inscribed upon a tablet in forgotten runes, with which my every movement, whether walking down our back steps left-foot-first or right-foot-first, must concur. Whatever my first inclination I decided against, because that lacked deliberateness.

Grandpa

I even avoided Grandpa Gallanti. He had a habit of walking up and down our lawn in the early evenings, for "inspection" as he called it, for "a breath of fresh air" as Mother said. But from the actual evidence of cigar butts which began to litter the yard in astonishing quantity, it was clear the only air Grandpa cared for was tobacco-flavored, and the only reason he stepped out at all was to spare Gram the misery of having to watch him shear years of his life away. Though Grandpa would undoubtedly have held that he had lived quite a while as it was, hence was beyond the danger of cutting his life short unless the shearing worked retroactively; in which case, smoking could only make him years younger.

One night Father was playing cribbage with Grandpa, who always called him McKiley instead of Macalpin as though he had forgotten his daughter's most recent suitor's name. Grandpa was whistling "Wolverton Mountain" and rattling his anise candy across his dentures with his lower lip for syncopation, like he always did when his dealt hand was so good that he would have enough left over for his crib, too, and Father grew a little short-tempered with me when I asked him about my present for the hundredth time.

He finally told me that, with all the cigar butts he had had to pick up off the yard lately, we didn't need a dog to litter it for us; thanks to a *certain person* he knew, we had as good as the real thing already. I knew Father was not serious, but he was upset; I also knew Grandpa did not really stand in the way of the pup I wanted. Still I felt I could take no chances, risk no bad luck, if my cantrip was to work perfectly. So I avoided Grandpa Gallanti for a few days.

Menace from above

Even his running war with Santa Claus lost all the fun it normally held for me. Neither ever won, because on Christmas day Grandpa, rubbing his eyes to get the sleep out, would walk from his room after most of the frenzied ripping of presents and Nance's shrieks were over, to see if anyone he knew "had gotten killed in the accident." Eventually, he made his way around our mess to the fireplace to check his stocking. In which he always found the same number of onions or potatoes we had seen him holding on Christmas Eve, when he announced we were all safe, because he intended to stand guard all night if necessary, but this year he was sure he could hit Santa (abdominous menace who burgled our house annually), not just one of his reindeer (Grandpa was usually able to potato the retreating Donder and Blitzen, and had once put out the bulb of Rudolph's nose). Grandpa's humor had a tendency towards bastinado Gram would check whenever she thought it too perverse, or when she saw his threats had begun to worry Nance and me.

Each year when we left Santa a tray of cookies and a glass of milk, Grandpa left a note:

> *Dear Big Pesty—You better enjoy these cookies while you can, because you gave me potatoes in my sock last year and I'm mad, and I saved all of them to throw back at you!*
>
> *Gino*

And each year Big Pesty answered, e.g.,

Fooey to you Gino—I stopped my reindeers across the street so you couldn't hit them if you tried. I know if you've been bad or good—and you are stinky—good-bye!

Nicky

P.S. And I told my reindeers to wee-wee on your car. Ho ho ho!

Upon finding first the note, and then the potatoes in his stocking the next day, Grandpa always went into an uproar, tearing the large cloth letter-holder (the shape and design of a Santa Claus), in which Mother kept all her Christmas cards, down from the fireplace with a loud rip of tape that made you think how much it would hurt to tear a band-aid off like that. Calling the letter-holder "Nicky" or "Big Pesty" or some other names Mother said were Italian, Grandpa held it upside down and whacked it several times from behind, causing its guts to spill over the carpet. Nance and I always laughed, attentive to these proceedings like kids at the smashing of a piñata, and not without similar interest, because after Grandpa had stomped off into the kitchen to begin his next offensive on Gram's coffeecake, Mother permitted us to take turns picking the cards we thought were the prettiest, and wanted to keep, off the floor.

A meditation

This year, I was too busy wanting a dog to think of anything else. Gram's thumbprint cookies, date cookies, and gingerbread left only a sort of pectin taste in my mouth and throat, and since I went to bed counting dogs instead of sheep and woke up thinking about more dogs, I wondered if I had slept at all in the interval. If so, then I must've had the same dream I did upon awakening.

Midnight reflections

It was the Christmas I couldn't wait. I went to sleep listening as always for faint sleigh-chimes upon the muffled night wind which blew frost in pagoda-shaped patterns across the window, but awoke instantaneously in the middle of the night, cold, and worrying about my pup. Because if he was not there under the tree, fine (or so I reasoned), but if he was, then he must be cold like me, and to let a puppy freeze on Christmas morning would be terrible, even a sin. As well as a disappointment, not to me—I didn't think a disappointment *to me*—but to the giver of the gift. I had another problem, of course. I stared at the dim ceiling of my and Nance's bedroom, which appeared to round over me like a light tent held suspended by my steady breathing; the tent always covering you when you are asleep and dreaming and which wakening rolls you away from, like a patient from the swathed-together clouds of the operating room. Nance made no noise in the next bed. If Santa had not come yet, then entering the living room to look for my pup would break the spell; Mother had told us to go to bed and stay there. The whole house was quiet. Outside the window, no wind blew hints of sleigh-bells.

All through the house

I arose feeling vulnerable. The invisible tent dissolved about me into infinite shards, the dim flecks of moonlight which half-melt, half-repel the darkness of early o'clocks and leave the interiors of rooms unfocused in a kind of black snow. I slipped out of the bedroom in my bathrobe, worn only when I was sick, or on holidays when I didn't want to waste any time getting dressed. Past Gram and Grandpa's room (Grandpa was snoring but suddenly faltered; irritably, I thought, as though in his sleep he was remembering past fights with Santa). Into the living room, accentuated with several fantastic shapes; and past the couch and TV stand, both oddly chiaroscuro in the half-darkness.

Then I remember being scared. An inflated punching clown that I guessed was for Nance smiled an eerie funhouse grin, and when I brushed past it, it suddenly rocked back and forth, taller than me.

On the other side of the heavily ornamented tree, glowing in a skylight moonbeam, appeared the head and tapering neck of a creature with no eyes and just a seam running across its mute face for a mouth. Most out of place was a feature which might have exaggerated it into a cartoon had the room been suddenly flooded with light, but now made it appear even more grotesque—a large cigar extending from its lips. The monster leered at me from off to one side of an amorphous pile of boxes, looking nothing at all like the outboard motor Mother and Father were planning to surprise Grandpa with for Christmas.

Disappointment and discovery

The pile of presents made my heart feel strange, then sink, not just because I knew I was cheating fate to be seeing it now, but because in the dark it looked much too big. I would have preferred to find a single, doghouse-sized box to the bigger heap which had always meant that, "Since Santa is sorry for all good little boys who are too young to be given a dog for Christmas, he has been a little extra kind to you this year." But I forgot all my past years' wishing and disappointment when I learned there was something in the room more frightened than me: from a spot nestled somewhere behind the pile of presents came a single muffled yelp.

Morning visitors

I had cheated her, but as she shook my shoulder the next morning, Nance was too excited to be angry because she had seen two heads sticking out from underneath my covers. One was a yellow-brown Sheltie's with a candy cane- striped ribbon in place of a collar. Grandpa came in wearing the floppy red drawers that made him look like Don Quixote in a Santa suit, and laughed. Father entered next and asked how I was. I told him I was fine, that my dog and I just wanted to sleep a while longer. So he left, but entered a minute later with his arm around Mother and holding the camera in his free hand. Mother smiled and asked me whether I wanted to get up now and open the rest of my presents with my little sister. I told her I did, but my dog was lying across me and if I moved, I would wake him up. Then Nance came to my rescue, carrying two large boxes in front of her, one hers and one mine, stacked so her staticky gold hair and sleepy eyes were just visible. It hadn't been much fun for her to open presents alone. I tried to open the first box as quietly as I could, but my hands trembled and tore the wrapping, and the pup awoke and wanted to play. So I let him help me attack the rest of the pile, shielding his eyes from the flash of Father's camera whenever I could, because that scared him.

Fox

I was completely happy for a week. Grandpa got his potatoes, but was so pleased with his new outboard motor and anxious to carry it down to the garage where he could practice racing it in our laundry tub that he nearly forgot to get mad at the letter-holder. When he dumped the guts out of it, as usual, adding the variation this year of thumping Nance's punching clown several times with his gnarled but powerful fists, I let my pup sniff the Christmas cards scattered on the floor and lick the ones that tasted best. I named him "Fox," not because he was wild or clever, but because I loved him, and he looked like a fox.

The shovel

The holiday spirit prevailed in our house right up until the episode with Mrs. Knowlan. When that hit, I caught up to the fact that the end of the year was closing fast and a reckoning had to be paid.

Snow fell and continued to fall towards the end of the week, and Father had been too busy using the shovel to remember where it had come from, too happily oblivious in his work that day to pay much attention to Mr. Knowlan, a couple of houses down, who had been standing knee-deep in his own driveway that afternoon, eyeing him suspiciously. But a month prior, Steve Eaves and I had begun digging a snow fort in a drift against the side of my garage, and Steve said we could use an extra shovel. Harry Knowlan materialized near us and offered to run to his house. When he returned, we allowed him to stay and help. The shovel stood leaning against the garage door at the end of the day. Even after the fort partially melted and Steve and I stomped on the cavern and crushed it, it remained like some forgotten monument of goodwill between Macalpins and Knowlans.

Where the wind blows

That day, Steve and I took my new dog outside for the first time so he could see where he lived, or learn about snow, or some such reason. The first thing Fox did was bolt down the street to the Knowlans' house. Hanging on their front porch was a set of wind chimes, three rows of tin triangles Mr. Knowlan brought back from Okinawa. I had heard Mother describe the noise of these chimes as "god-awful," but Fox was an undiscriminating puppy always bursting around to investigate things before considering the actual danger to himself (I would spend a great deal of time trying to keep him from trying to nip at the cars that invaded our street over those first months). Or perhaps there was a finer sphery music to the chimes that our ears couldn't accommodate, but his could, because when Steve and I caught up to him, he was howling along in earnest.

Neighborhood witch

Mrs. Knowlan came to the door and looked down at Fox, and then slowly, at us. To Steve and I, she was the closest thing in the world to a witch. She had red-rimmed eyes and a stare that made you think evil eyes came in pairs. Her skin looked drained of blood, or maybe it was sun, because she had a mild Alabama twang which would have been innocuous enough, or even pleasant I suppose, had she not always spoken with such deathly insistency. We usually spotted her out in her yard in summer wearing an enormous straw hat and shorts that exposed her pale legs. Once I heard my mother and Mrs. Eaves giggling in the alleyway as they snuck peeks at Mrs. Knowlan at work in her garden. She looked as though she was trying to stare away the weeds.

A social call

Steve and I immediately felt ourselves in a hurry when Mrs. Knowlan came to the door. But to make the best of things—that is, to explain our presence there—we had to do something we hadn't done before. We called for Harry.

If you had told me two minutes before Steve and I were going to call for him, I would have been almost as surprised as if you had told me that, shortly afterwards, Harry would be playing cribbage with Grandpa. But he was. We were able to fetch Fox back to my yard, though it was necessary to drag him most of the way. Once there, the first things to attract his attention were the swirling snowflakes, but then he found more dangerous game. He began sniffing and gnawing Grandpa's cigar butts.

I worried desperately that Fox would become sick on what would have been an all-day feast, but couldn't get him to leave the stubs alone. So into the house he had to go. Steve and I wouldn't have hesitated to follow Fox, but then we remembered Harry, who had not ceased grinning since we had called for him at his house. He had never been in my house except for one early birthday party, but since it was not the case that he had invited himself over, the situation placed a demand on my conscience I hadn't faced before, either.

And though I would not have admitted it to Steve, I hadn't quite figured out what was wrong with Harry, beyond his name perhaps, or his eyes that were beginning to crave spectacles. I felt sorry for him. I heard Fox yipping inside and my heart filled with generosity. I told Harry he could come in if he wanted.

Surprise guest

I hadn't stopped to consider what my mother would think. She walked to the door to keep Fox (who immediately tried to get back out) from scratching it. For a while, she was too preoccupied to count the heads coming in, only telling us to take our boots off on the door mat if we valued our lives.

Maybe it was the sound six boots make when they are unbuckled and squeaked off that was too much for her, in retrospect. Because she eventually looked over, startled, as though expecting to find Steve and I had sprouted another leg apiece just to spite her, to add to her winter-long struggle to keep the front hallway sandbagged with rugs.

For a brief second she paused, in a surprised but slightly amused silence, as she looked from me to Steve to Harry, who grinned.

I needn't have worried, though. Mother's holiday spirit was more indomitable than usual that year and could extend itself even to the Knowlans. She fell back upon her social instinct and offered Harry some Christmas cookies.

"Gosh, that'd be swell, Mrs. Macalpin," said Harry. And that was all. In fact, Harry's presence among us held nothing of what it might have had he been a notorious outlaw or an apostate rather than the lonely kid from down the block who had left his shovel propped against our garage for a whole month.

Nosy Nance

Harry divided most of his stay between watching Steve and me trying to teach Fox to shake hands and watching TV with Gram and Nance, who amused herself by telling him she saw something green and he had to guess it, but lying and shaking her head every time Harry said the Christmas tree, and then she made Harry repeat "I shot the city sheriff," because that made you say the *S*-word, but Harry pronounced all the words impeccably, so that shut her up.

Nance's narrative

Father got up to shovel the driveway, choosing to face snow and wind as more clement alternatives to losing to Grandpa again. Grandpa was still sitting at the table growing bored with cheating himself at game after game of solitaire (he called it "solitary," a name which possibly reflected his view that it was a game only fit for a man in confinement). He told Harry he sounded like an intelligent sort of young fellow and asked him whether he knew how to play cribbage. Harry didn't, but characteristically, said he would like to learn.

What followed then, according to Nance, who didn't find anything to interest her on the TV (neither had Gram, who had fallen asleep on her chair), and who was jealous of all the attention I and especially Steve had been paying to the dog and nothing else lately, and so had islanded herself on Grandpa's lap for comfort because he would sing "I Can't Give You Anything But Love, Baby" to her—what followed then was that Harry proceeded to beat the pants off Grandpa. It is hard enough to imagine Grandpa Gallanti having to swallow defeat, but it is harder still to picture him having to lose to someone like Harry, who had to lay his hands down on the table and ask if they were good. I did notice Grandpa started to crunch his anise candy rather than rattle it, and after a while stopped singing. Instead, he shifted Nance off his lap to devote his full attention to the little boy across the table by whom he was being double-skunked. His pupil, of whom he had asked *Capisco?* while explaining the rules of the game. Now the most he could muster was a dry "Cripers!" and a *sotto voce,* "Ay-yi-yi."

The first round

I never saw my Grandfather Gallanti double-skunked in a game of cribbage in my life, although if my father had had him where Harry did, what happened next would never have been permitted as an interruption. This being the first of Mrs. Knowlan's phone calls.

The contrast between my mother's voice, full of good cheer and tinged with holiday-nog, and Mrs. Knowlan's, cold, curt, and serious, must have been disconcerting to any operator who might have been listening. At the time, I could only follow half of the conversation, naturally, but I was able to fill in the blanks shortly afterwards, when my mother, after hanging up with Mrs. Knowlan, angrily dialed Mrs. Eaves to replay the whole thing back. In this account, she enacted Mrs. Knowlan's half of the conversation herself, complete with Southern twang.

While over the years many additions were made to accounts of this conversation, over numerous family retellings, I still tend to trust the general accuracy of that first folio version presented to Mrs. Eaves.

"I can't find my son Harry," said the voice on the other end of the phone. "He doesn't answer when I call."

"He is here with Jim and Steve. Shall I send him home?"

"*What?*" (Mrs. Knowlan could not have expected this).

"He is here with Jim and Steve," Mother repeated. "Do you want him sent home now?"

The voice on the other end faltered.

"I wondered where he was. Yes. The other day Harry came home smelling of cigarettes. I can't have him smoking with the neighborhood boys."

Mrs. Knowlan tended to talk in a string of statement-making sentences a logical positivist would have loved, but her change of subject here is admittedly somewhat baffling.

"Are you saying that it was with *my* boy that Harry was smoking?" Mother replied, loudly enough for Fox to prick up his ears.

Steve and I tensed, because a few weeks ago he had picked up one of Grandpa's less-finished cigar butts and dared Harry, who had tagged along after us, to smoke it. Harry did, but then afterwards looked a little sick.

"Your boy? I don't know."

I never ascertained whether Mrs. Knowlan learned to distinguish any of us children; or rather, if she saw us as members of a neighborhood junta of boys at constant war with hers.

"Harry said the boys find cigar butts in people's yards and smoke them. But I won't have my son smoking. He was to stay around the yard today. He was being punished."

"I'll have a talk with my boy, Susan. If he is the one who made Harry try a cigar butt, then he is going to be punished, too."

"I wondered where he was," said Mrs. Knowlan, almost kindly.

"Yes. Goodbye," Mother told her. "James!"

"I have to go," Steve Eaves whispered.

Sudden impulse

I wished that I could go, too. I had a sudden impulse: my dog was with me and I didn't want him to be scared like I was, but more importantly, I didn't want to be reprimanded in front of him for I reason I couldn't explain, call it guilt or shame, or the fact that Fox was my friend, whose liking and respect must be safeguarded, and Mother's calls were a summons into a family realm whence friends like Steve and Fox and sometimes Grandpa were to be winnowed in reverse: they were the good, and I was the chaff.

"Whyn't you take Fox out for a walk," I suggested hopefully to Steve. "I'll come out as soon as I can."

"*James Macalpin!*" Mother repeated.

"Harry," she added, as if in afterthought.

I could hear the bang of the front door that meant Steve had made a quick exit with Fox, and felt abandoned. Harry pushed his chair back from the table and Grandpa beat a retreat, not just from Harry but from Mother, who sooner or later would come around to the question of the cigar butts. I was glad to see him, like Steve, escape.

Tagalong

Harry followed me out into the kitchen.

"Your mother called," mine said. Then she turned to me.

"Have you been smoking?

"No."

"Has he?"

Harry came to the rescue when I paused. "Yes, ma'am, and I'm sorry, ma'am."

Mother questioned him now. "Has Jim been smoking?"

"No, Mrs. Macalpin," Harry replied graciously. "Just me."

That was true as far as he knew; the other day we had settled for double-daring Harry, though a year ago Steve and I had tried smoking and hadn't liked it, and to hide the smell on our breath we walked to the Handy Pantry and bought a bottle of mouthwash from a teenage girl who asked which of us had the date. And then we had gotten even sicker on the mouthwash than we had on the cigar, because we hadn't known you were supposed to swish it in your mouth and spit it out, like toothpaste, so we drank it down instead, because it tasted like maraschino cherries.

"Did he—or did Steve—give you a cigar butt to smoke?"

Harry would rather have bared himself to a year's spankings than tattle, but now he was torn, because unlike any normal kid he had never learned to lie. So he answered, "Steve did," sparing me.

Second round

My mother relaxed a little, and might even have recaptured her holiday spirit if the phone hadn't rung again, summoning her like a bell for the next round.

"A dog is in my yard. Is it yours?" rasped Mrs. Knowlan.

"We don't have a dog—wait," my mother snapped. "Jim, where is your dog?"

"Steve took him out," I answered, starting to panic and feeling as though all the magic of the past week was dissipating, snaking back into its bottle to be recapped. "Mom, Fox!" I yelled. "Those wind chimes!"

"What wind chimes?"

"Knowlan's wind chimes! Fox likes them!" I told her how Fox had bolted off to the Knowlan's yard earlier that day, and started to blubber.

"Well, stop it. We'll get your dog back," she reassured me.

"My husband is getting his air rifle."

"I hope-that-won't-be-necessary," Mother replied, her fury spelling itself out through tight lips.

"Why was Harry not sent home?" the voice countered.

My mother looked over at Harry. She had forgotten about him.

"Harry, your mother wants you," she said, thinking out loud.

I had gone so wild with worry I punched Harry, hard, on the arm. "Go!" I yelled. "Get out-a here!"

A hostage situation

But then Mother had her sudden inspiration. And I began to realize that sometimes you not only have to whittle out what you want, but the going-about-the-thing can provide a keener pleasure than the actual getting.

At the same time my mother was being furious at Mrs. Knowlan, whether aware of it or not, she was beginning to savor the battle a little.

All I knew was that I loved my dog and wanted him back, *now*. Because holding him at that moment would have erased the anxiety I was feeling, instantly. I couldn't understand how she could want Fox back, like me, but not appear to be in any hurry.

Why, instead, she chose to negotiate.

"Wait," she said. "Wait just a minute," she repeated, stalling the voice on the phone and everyone else.

"Mrs. Knowlan, I'd be happy to send Harry home just as soon as my boy's dog is home safely."

When she said that, I wasn't sure whether I should still be mad at Harry or not—not just because guilt over hitting him had struck me back, but also because he might turn out to be a valuable stake in this game.

Harry, at mention of his name, braved a smile.

The negotiations

Mother was now in high gear. She opened the negotiations by apologizing to Mrs. Knowlan (Catherine) for being so blunt, but explained how I had wanted a dog for years and years, and how this Christmas, against her better judgment perhaps, I had gotten one, which I adored and had never let out of my sight before, as far as she knew. She even threw in the story of how the family found me in bed with the puppy on Christmas morning, how everyone had gathered around my bed to unwrap presents and pet him.

As I listened to this narrative, I suddenly began to feel a bit self-conscious while standing there next to Harry, who was smiling and saying, "Neat!"

Mrs. Knowlan then retracted her earlier remark about the air rifle, or rather stated it would no longer be necessary, because she saw a boy standing at the edge of her lawn with a leash in his hands. She would permit him to come up on her porch to capture the animal instead.

Negotiations, continued

Had my mother been content with Mrs. Knowlan's rapprochement, everything might have worked out smoothly at this point, and an armistice between Macalpins and Knowlans achieved. But she was not yet satisfied—the harder negotiations were about to begin.

"Just one more thing," she said. "A moment ago you accused my boy of forcing Harry to smoke. Harry told me that it was not my son, but another boy who encouraged him."

"Which boy is that?" Mrs. Knowlan rasped.

This put my mother in an uncomfortable position because she was friends with Steve's mother. But righteousness triumphed.

"Steve Eaves."

The voice on the other end of the line hesitated. Perhaps the controlling consciousness there was deliberating over whether to take the easy route and apologize or tread the hard road of truth a little further.

"I did not accuse your boy in particular, but aren't Steve Eaves and your son always together? Are you saying James wasn't there when it happened?"

"That's not the point!" my mother yelled, her ire now thoroughly aroused. "You had no right to accuse my boy!"

"But I never did accuse your son."

Then my mother got tough. Perhaps she felt that she had to rebut Mrs. Knowlan's remark about me and Steve always being together. I had to look away, watching Harry buckle on his boots.

"If you have any complaints about the other day, then you should talk to Joanne Eaves. But Steve is a good boy. After all, it wasn't him, but Harry who tried the cigar. Had *my* boy done such a thing I wouldn't be so quick to point the finger at the other neighborhood kids.

"To think that Jim and Steve have been playing nicely with Harry all afternoon, too, and he has been sitting around my house eating Christmas cookies, and you call me up and accuse my son of corrupting him over something that happened Lord knows how long ago."

Harry was sobbing.

My mother was triumphant. She really felt she had Mrs. Knowlan backed into a corner now.

Trump card

But Susan Knowlan had not yet played her ace-in-the-hole; her final trump. In so doing, she suddenly brought into the picture my poor father, who at that moment had just finished clearing our driveway with the Knowlan shovel. He had seen it by the garage so often it became imprinted in his mind as his own. Mother had to shout out the door for him, then ultimately send Grandpa (who was too gun-shy of his daughter's wrath to even consider a smoke) down the yard to fetch it.

An ending

In the end, we had it all worked out with Mrs. Knowlan. We swapped Harry and the shovel for Fox, and since the wind chimes also disappeared from the Knowlan porch for a while, the overall balance of trade was probably even. But Mother had come within the shovel of winning, and never really forgave Harry's mom for that.

I had my dog back, safe, which would have been all that mattered to me only minutes before; but now left me with mixed feelings, a little cautious, because I had just learned how the loved things of the world may be lost in the transaction.

ACKNOWLEDGMENTS

My thanks to the editors of *Bank-Heavy Press, Bluepepper, Connotations Press, Epiphany, Ink Monkey Press, Midwestern Gothic, The Monarch Review,* and *Numinous,* in which several of these pieces originally appeared.

ABOUT THE AUTHOR

M.V. Montgomery is a native of Minneapolis who has lived and taught in Arizona and Georgia for over twenty-five years. He is the author of two previous poetry collections, the British release *Joshu Holds a Press Conference*, and *Strange Conveyances*, which *Muscle & Blood* magazine named best poetry book of 2010. His creative work has appeared in dozens of literary journals and e-zines, and his fiction has also been nominated by editors for Pushcart and PEN/Faulkner awards. A professor at Life University, he lives in the Atlanta area with his family.

photo by Ada Montgomery

Follow M.V. Montgomery on his website: *mvmontgomery.wordpress.com*